Aya Weiss

Antarctica Cruise

Travel Guide

Catalog

Welcome to the Antarctica Cruise Expedition

Exploring Antarctica: A Pristine Odyssey

Antarctica, often referred to as the "White Continent," stands as a testament to the beauty and wonders of the natural world. As you embark on this cruise, you'll find yourself immersed in a world of breathtaking landscapes, wildlife, and scientific discoveries that will leave you in awe.

Ushuaia: The Gateway to the Frozen Continent

Ushuaia, the southernmost city in the world, is the starting point of your journey to Antarctica. Located at the tip of South America, this charming town offers a unique blend of Patagonian culture and stunning natural beauty. Explore the Tierra del Fuego National Park, known for its rugged terrain and diverse wildlife. Prepare to set sail on your expedition to the frozen wonderland of Antarctica.

Antarctic Peninsula: A Frozen Paradise

As your cruise reaches the Antarctic Peninsula, you'll be surrounded by a pristine wilderness of ice and snow. Marvel at the towering icebergs and glaciers that seem to stretch endlessly into the horizon. Keep your binoculars ready to spot penguins, seals, and various seabirds that call this region home.

Visit research stations where scientists are unlocking the mysteries of this remote continent.

Antarctic Wildlife Encounters

Throughout your cruise, prepare to encounter the extraordinary wildlife of Antarctica. Observe majestic humpback whales breaching the icy waters, witness colonies of thousands of Adélie and Gentoo penguins, and be amazed by the graceful movements of leopard seals. Your journey through this remote wilderness is a rare opportunity to connect with nature at its most untouched.

Scientific Exploration and Conservation Efforts

Learn about the vital research conducted in Antarctica to better understand climate change, glaciology, and marine biology. Participate in citizen science programs and gain insights into the ongoing efforts to protect this fragile environment. Your voyage also supports conservation initiatives aimed at preserving the pristine beauty of Antarctica for future generations.

Captivating Icescapes and Remote Wonders

As your cruise navigates through Antarctica's frigid waters, you'll be treated to ever-changing ice formations and incredible landscapes. From the serene beauty of Lemaire Channel to the towering cliffs of the Antarctic Sound, the region offers postcard-perfect vistas at every turn. Keep your camera ready as you witness breathtaking sunsets over the ice-covered horizon and the ethereal glow of the polar lights.

This Antarctica Cruise promises a pristine odyssey that immerses you in the natural beauty, wildlife encounters, and scientific wonders of the frozen continent. Every day offers a new adventure, making this journey a true voyage of discovery through one of the most remarkable and remote places on Earth.

Antarctica Cruise's Top 10 Must-Visit Destinations

1. Antarctic Peninsula:

- **History:** The Antarctic Peninsula has long been a focus of exploration and scientific research. Early navigators, including James Cook, sighted the Peninsula in the 18th century, but it wasn't until the late 19th and early 20th centuries that expeditions like Shackleton's and Amundsen's began to make history here. In more recent times, it has become a hub for scientific research, with numerous research stations studying climate change and glaciology. Today, it's a critical area for understanding the impacts of global warming on the polar regions.

- **Key Attractions:** Look out for unique species like the Antarctic penguin, orca, and leopard seals. Witness massive icebergs calving from glaciers.

- **When to Visit**: Cruise operators typically offer expeditions from November to March when wildlife is most active and the weather is relatively mild.

- **Hidden Gems**: Explore the Lemaire Channel, known for its pristine beauty and perfect photogenic moments.
- **Culinary Delights:** Enjoy gourmet meals aboard your cruise, often featuring international and regional cuisine.

2. South Georgia Island:

- **History:** South Georgia Island, with its rich history of exploration, gained prominence as a hub for the sealing and whaling industries in the 18th and 19th centuries. It played a pivotal role in the story of Ernest Shackleton's survival journey after his ship, the Endurance, was crushed by ice. Now, South Georgia is a wildlife haven, known for its spectacular penguin colonies, seals, and a variety of seabirds, attracting wildlife enthusiasts from around the world.
- **Key Attractions:** South Georgia is home to the world's largest king penguin colony at St. Andrews Bay. It's also known for Grytviken, an abandoned whaling station.
- **When to Visit:** The austral summer is the best time to visit when the island comes to life with wildlife and accessible weather.

- **Hidden Gems:** Explore the remote beaches of Gold Harbor, where elephant seals and fur seals bask in the sun.
- **Culinary Delights**: Experience local British cuisine on your cruise with a blend of international flavors.

3. Lemaire Channel:

- **History:** The Lemaire Channel was first explored by the German expedition of 1873-74, led by Eduard Dallmann, who named it after Charles Lemaire, a Belgian explorer. This dramatic passage was frequently used by whalers and sealers in the early 20th century, and its narrowness and towering cliffs have made it a renowned scenic spot for modern-day Antarctic cruises.
- **Key Attractions**: The Lemaire Channel is famous for its dramatic, narrow passage between towering cliffs, making it a photographer's paradise.
- **When to Visit:** The channel is traversed during your Antarctica cruise, providing awe-inspiring vistas.
- **Fascinating Fact**: The channel is often nicknamed the "Kodak Gap" due to its sheer photogenic beauty.

4. Paradise Bay:

- **History:** Paradise Bay has been a site of scientific interest for decades. Its stunning glaciers and unique geology have attracted researchers studying climate change and glaciology. The bay's name reflects its awe-inspiring beauty and tranquil environment, making it a paradise for wildlife enthusiasts and photographers.

- **Key Attractions:** Paradise Bay offers a chance to witness diverse wildlife like seals, whales, and a variety of seabirds against the backdrop of serene glaciers.

- **When to Visit:** The austral summer months of November to March are ideal for visiting this pristine bay.

- **Fascinating Fact:** It's named Paradise Bay for a reason – the breathtaking scenery and peaceful surroundings truly make it a paradise for explorers.

5. Half Moon Island:

- **History:** Half Moon Island has a history tied to early whaling and sealing activities. Remnants of these industries can still be seen on the island. Now, it's a protected area and part of the South Shetland Islands, providing a glimpse into Antarctica's history while showcasing its natural beauty and wildlife.

- **Key Attractions**: This small island is home to a thriving colony of chinstrap penguins and provides picturesque views of Livingston Island.

- **When to Visit:** Explore the island during the austral summer when wildlife is most active.

- **Hidden Gems:** Keep an eye out for striking views of the South Shetland Islands on the horizon.

6. Paulet Island:

- **History**: Paulet Island's history is intertwined with the era of exploration and sealing. It served as a base for early Antarctic expeditions, and evidence of these activities remains in the form of hut ruins. Today, it stands as a testament to the explorers of the past and a vital habitat for Adélie penguins and other wildlife.

- **Key Attractions:** Paulet Island is famed for its large Adélie penguin colony and the presence of a dormant volcanic cone.

- **When to Visit:** The austral summer months provide the best opportunity to explore the island's unique landscapes.

- **Fascinating Fact:** The island's volcanic history adds an extra layer of intrigue to the surrounding icy wilderness.

7. Ross Ice Shelf:

- **History:** Named after British explorer Sir James Clark Ross, the Ross Ice Shelf has been a focus of scientific research for over a century. Captain Robert Falcon Scott's ill-fated Terra Nova Expedition used it as a base, and scientific study of its ice has helped us understand Antarctica's vital role in global climate systems.

- **Key Attractions**: Discover the immense scale of this ice shelf, which plays a vital role in regulating global sea levels.

- **When to Visit:** Your cruise typically sails close to the Ross Ice Shelf during the Antarctic summer.

- **Fascinating Fact**: It's the world's largest ice shelf, covering an area larger than Spain.

8. Aitcho Islands:

- **History:** The Aitcho Islands have a history of being visited by early explorers and sealers in the 19th century. These islands were named after Lieutenant Commander Aitcho of the Imperial Russian Navy, who surveyed the region in 1912. Today, they are known for their biodiversity, offering opportunities to observe a variety of wildlife in their natural habitats.

- **Key Attractions:** The Aitcho Islands offer opportunities for wildlife encounters, from penguins to seals and various bird species.

- **When to Visit:** The austral summer season provides the best conditions for exploring the islands.

- **Hidden Gems**: Delight in the sights and sounds of countless seabirds that nest on these remote islands.

9. Drake Passage:

- History: The Drake Passage is named after Sir Francis Drake, the English sea captain, who sailed these waters in the late 16th century. It has long been a challenging yet exhilarating route for mariners. Now, it's a gateway for modern Antarctic exploration, offering a thrilling, if at times tempestuous, experience for visitors.

- Key Attractions: Though known for its rough waters, the Drake Passage offers an incredible chance to observe marine life, including albatrosses and petrels.

- When to Visit: You'll cross the Drake Passage as part of your cruise expedition to Antarctica.

- Fascinating Fact: This legendary passage marks the transition from the southernmost tip of South America to the pristine landscapes of Antarctica.

10. Falkland Islands:

- History: The Falkland Islands have a complex history marked by disputes between the UK and Argentina. Originally settled by the French in the 18th century, the islands later became a British colony. In 1982, the Falklands War erupted between the UK and Argentina, ending with British sovereignty. Today, the islands are known for their rich wildlife and are a popular destination for wildlife enthusiasts and history buffs alike.

   - **Key Attractions**: The islands are teeming with wildlife, including colonies of penguins and diverse landscapes for exploration.

   - **When to Visit:** The austral summer (November to March) provides the most favorable conditions for a visit.

   - **Fascinating Fact:** The Falkland Islands offer a unique blend of British and South American influences, evident in their culture and cuisine.

Culinary Delights: While aboard your Antarctica cruise, savor the flavors of the region, often including fresh seafood, international cuisine, and carefully curated menus designed to enhance your polar expedition experience.

Please note *that the destinations you'll visit during your Antarctica cruise may vary depending on your chosen cruise line and its specific itinerary. Cruise lines have set schedules and predetermined ports of call.*

I recommend contacting your chosen cruise line to obtain a comprehensive list of all the destinations included in your cruise itinerary. This will help you plan and ensure you don't miss out on any potential new and exciting locations along your journey.

Need to Know

- **Visas**: Visitors to Antarctica typically don't require visas as the region is governed by the Antarctic Treaty System. Verify specific requirements based on your nationality and itinerary.
- **Mobile Phones:** Ensure your mobile phone is set to roaming mode for uninterrupted connectivity. Local SIM cards may be available at your embarkation point.
- **Time:** Be aware of time zone differences as you cross various countries and regions during your cruise. It's essential for scheduling activities and making travel arrangements.
- **Seasons**: Antarctica experiences distinct seasons:
  - *High Season (Nov–Feb)*: The austral summer offers the best wildlife viewing opportunities, with abundant penguins and seals.
  - *Shoulder Season (Mar & Oct)*: Early and late austral summer provide quieter cruises with reasonable prices.
  - *Low Season (Apr–Sep)*: During the austral winter, you can witness breathtaking ice formations and serene landscapes. It's a challenging time for tourism due to harsh weather conditions.
- **Emergency Numbers:** In case of emergencies during your Antarctica cruise, remember these essential contact numbers:
  - *Ship Crew:* The ship's crew will be your primary contact for onboard emergencies.
  - *Expedition Leaders*: Reach out to expedition leaders for guidance and assistance during excursions.
  - *Emergency Evacuation*: In extreme cases, the vessel's crew will coordinate emergency evacuations. Follow their instructions.

First Time on an Antarctica Cruise?

What to Wear:

Antarctica's unique environment calls for specific clothing choices. Be prepared for varying weather conditions, including cold temperatures, strong winds, and potential rain. Here are some tips on what to wear:

Layered Clothing: Dress in layers to adjust to changing weather conditions. Thermal base layers, insulated jackets, and waterproof outerwear are essential.

Waterproof Gear: Bring waterproof pants and boots to keep dry during Zodiac landings and onshore activities.

Warm Accessories: Don't forget essentials like gloves, scarves, warm hats, and sunglasses for protection against the cold and sun.

Sturdy Footwear: Insulated and waterproof boots are crucial for wet landings and shore excursions on icy terrain.

Sleeping:

Accommodations on your Antarctica cruise will be provided by the cruise line. Cabins can range from standard to luxurious, depending on your preferences and budget. Cruise ships may offer various amenities, dining options, and guided shore excursions in each port of call.

What to Pack:

For a comfortable and enjoyable Antarctica cruise, consider packing the following:

Travel Adapters: Ensure you have the appropriate electrical adapters to charge your devices.

Clothing for Activities: Pack attire suitable for the activities you plan to engage in during shore excursions, including cold-weather gear and waterproof clothing.

Cruise Documents: Bring all necessary travel documents, such as your passport, visa (if required), and cruise itinerary.

Medications and Essentials: Carry any prescription medications, over-the-counter remedies, and toiletries to ensure you're well-prepared for your journey.

Money: Most expenses are covered in your Antarctica cruise package. However, having some local currency for personal expenses during shore excursions or in ports of call is useful. Credit cards are widely accepted on cruise ships, but notify your bank of your travel plans to avoid potential card usage issues.

Etiquette:

Navigating your Antarctica cruise with respect for the environment and local customs is crucial. Here are some etiquette tips to help you enjoy your journey with courtesy:

Environmental Responsibility: Follow all environmental guidelines set by the cruise line to preserve the pristine Antarctic environment.

Respect Cultural Norms: When visiting research stations or local communities, be mindful of their customs and traditions. Follow any specific guidelines provided by your cruise line.

Hiking

Antarctica offers stunning hiking opportunities amidst its pristine landscapes, where you can explore the unique beauty of the frozen continent. Here are some hiking options:

- **Antarctic Peninsula:** Hike through the breathtaking landscapes of the Antarctic Peninsula, featuring glaciers, ice formations, and stunning vistas. The best time for hiking is during the austral summer (Nov–Feb).

- **South Georgia Island:** Discover the rugged terrain of South Georgia Island, known for its rich wildlife and historical sites. Hiking here is most enjoyable during the austral summer months.

Canoeing and Kayaking

Paddling in the icy waters surrounding Antarctica provides a unique perspective on its diverse landscapes. Options include:

- Antarctic Peninsula: Explore serene bays, witness wildlife, and get up close to icebergs while kayaking around the Antarctic Peninsula.

Rock Climbing

For those seeking a unique challenge, consider rock climbing on nearby islands or in Patagonia. While not in Antarctica itself, these locations offer thrilling rock climbing experiences.

- Patagonia: Patagonia, in southern South America, provides excellent rock climbing opportunities amidst its stunning natural scenery.

Best Times to Go:

- Antarctica Cruise (Nov–Feb): The austral summer offers the best conditions for activities like hiking, kayaking, and wildlife watching in Antarctica.

Choosing Cruise for Adventure Activities:

- Some Antarctica cruise itineraries may offer adventure activities like kayaking or other water-based excursions. Check with the cruise company to learn about the specific activities available and ensure they align with your interests and fitness level.
- It's important to note that activities like kayaking in Antarctica may require prior experience or training, so inquire with the cruise line about any prerequisites.
- While Antarctica offers limited adventure activities due to its extreme environment, your cruise may include opportunities for active exploration in the surrounding regions of South America.
Embracing adventure activities in and around Antarctica allows you to experience the awe-inspiring landscapes and unique wildlife of this remote region while staying active and engaged throughout your journey.

Ancient Myth and Speculation

The history of Antarctica traces its roots to the realm of myth and speculation in the ancient world. Although the Greeks and Romans, with their exploration and knowledge of the known world, did not venture as far south as Antarctica, they were aware of the concept of a southern landmass. Ancient philosophers and geographers like Aristotle, Ptolemy, and Strabo theorized about the existence of a southern continent, and they referred to it as "Terra Australis Incognita" or the "Unknown Southern Land."

In the Middle Ages and the early Renaissance, these ideas persisted. Maps from this era often featured an expansive southern landmass, although its actual existence remained unproven. It wasn't until the Age of Exploration in the 15th and 16th centuries that seafarers began their journeys in search of this enigmatic southern continent.

Early European Exploration

The early exploration of Antarctica was marked by a series of voyages undertaken by European navigators. Portuguese explorer Ferdinand Magellan, on his circumnavigation of the Earth in the early 16th century, ventured into the Southern Ocean and may have sighted the northern reaches of the Antarctic Peninsula. However, he did not recognize the landmass as a continent.

The real push to explore Antarctica came with the age of great navigators like James Cook, who made several voyages to the South Pacific and the Southern Ocean in the late 18th century. Cook's expeditions extended knowledge of the southern seas but still did not provide conclusive evidence of the continent's existence.

The Nineteenth Century - Early Antarctic Exploration

The 19th century marked the beginning of more systematic and focused exploration of the Antarctic region. Sealers and whalers were among the first to venture into Antarctic waters. They were primarily drawn by the prospect of hunting seals and whales for their valuable resources. These early expeditions established some of the first known landings on the continent, even though they were often accidental or for economic purposes rather than scientific exploration.

The early 19th century also saw explorers like William Smith and Edward Bransfield, who sailed in the vicinity of the Antarctic Peninsula, making some of the first confirmed sightings of the continent. Nevertheless, it was still unclear whether Antarctica was a large landmass or a series of islands.

The Heroic Age of Antarctic Exploration

The early 20th century, often referred to as the "Heroic Age of Antarctic Exploration," witnessed a significant increase in expeditions aimed at unraveling the mysteries of Antarctica. This era saw several iconic explorers and expeditions, and their endeavors form a crucial part of Antarctica's history.

One of the most famous figures of this period was Sir Ernest Shackleton, whose expeditions, particularly the Endurance Expedition of 1914-1917, are etched in history as tales of resilience and survival in the harshest of conditions. Shackleton's ship, the Endurance, became trapped in the ice, leading to an incredible story of survival as he and his crew endured a harrowing ordeal in their quest to return home.

Discovery of the South Pole

A major milestone in Antarctic exploration was reached when Norwegian explorer Roald Amundsen and his team became the first to reach the South Pole in December 1911, beating British explorer Robert Falcon Scott's expedition by a few weeks. Amundsen's achievement marked a defining moment in the history of Antarctic exploration and cemented the presence of a significant landmass at the southernmost tip of the world.

The history of Antarctica unfolds as a tale of continued exploration, scientific research, and international collaboration. As we move forward, we explore the mid-20th century, the establishment of research stations, and the challenges of sovereignty in Antarctica.

Post-World War II Era and Scientific Research

After the turbulent years of World War II, scientific exploration of Antarctica took on a more prominent role. The war had seen many nations cooperating on various fronts, and this spirit of collaboration extended to the scientific study of the southern continent. The international community recognized the potential of Antarctica as a place for valuable research.

In 1957, the International Geophysical Year (IGY) was launched, a cooperative scientific effort involving 12 countries. During the IGY, research stations were established in Antarctica, and scientific exploration thrived. The year 1957 was also significant for the launch of Sputnik, the world's first artificial satellite, by the Soviet Union. This event marked the beginning of the space race and further propelled scientific interest in the Antarctic for its unique insights into Earth's environment.

The Antarctic Treaty System

The mounting scientific interest in Antarctica brought with it the need to address questions of territorial sovereignty and to ensure that the region remained a zone of international cooperation. This led to the negotiation and signing of the Antarctic Treaty on December 1, 1959. The treaty established Antarctica as a region dedicated to peace and science. It prohibited military activities and nuclear testing while promoting cooperation among the signatory nations.

The Antarctic Treaty laid the groundwork for a unique governance system in Antarctica. It was an unprecedented achievement in international diplomacy, and it set a standard for environmental protection that would become increasingly relevant in the later decades of the 20th century.

Cold War and Research Stations

The years of the Cold War saw a significant increase in the number of research stations established on the continent. The United States, the Soviet Union, and other nations constructed research facilities, including the famed American McMurdo Station and the Soviet Vostok Station. Research on Antarctica became an arena for demonstrating technological and scientific prowess.

The scientific work conducted in Antarctica extended beyond meteorology and geology. It encompassed a wide range of disciplines, including biology, glaciology, oceanography, and climate science. The continent provided a unique laboratory for understanding the Earth's climate and ecosystems, as well as the broader implications for global environmental issues.

Environmental Concerns and Conservation Efforts

As the world became increasingly aware of environmental issues, Antarctica was not exempt from these concerns. The pristine and fragile nature of the continent's ecosystems led to growing international efforts to protect its environment. The Madrid Protocol, an amendment to the Antarctic Treaty, was adopted in 1991. It designated Antarctica as a natural reserve, prohibited mineral resource activities, and established environmental principles for human activities on the continent.

The Protocol also called for the comprehensive protection of the Antarctic environment and recognized the need to prevent pollution. These conservation efforts were a response to growing concerns about the impact of human activities on Antarctica's unique ecosystems and the consequences of climate change.

Modern Exploration and Scientific Research

In the 21st century, Antarctica remains a hub for scientific research. Research stations from various nations are continually occupied, and the knowledge gained from the continent continues to inform our understanding of the Earth's climate and environment. Issues like sea level rise, the melting of polar ice, and the effects of climate change are increasingly prominent topics of research in Antarctica.

International cooperation remains a key feature of Antarctica's history. The Antarctic Treaty System, which now includes over 50 signatory nations, stands as a testament to the ability of nations to work together for the common good. Antarctica remains a symbol of international collaboration, a place of scientific discovery, and a crucial region for understanding the planet's changing environment.

As we continue our journey through the history of Antarctica, we explore contemporary challenges, international agreements, and the ongoing research that continues to shape our understanding of this frozen continent.

Contemporary Challenges and Environmental Concerns

Antarctica faces numerous contemporary challenges, primarily related to the impact of human activities and climate change. While the Antarctic Treaty and its associated agreements have done much to protect the region, the continent is not immune to the pressures of a changing world.

One of the most pressing concerns is climate change. Antarctica is particularly sensitive to global temperature increases, and the warming of the continent has far-reaching implications. The retreat of glaciers and the collapse of ice shelves are occurring at an accelerated pace, leading to rising sea levels and significant changes in the region's ecosystems.

Scientific research in Antarctica plays a critical role in understanding these changes and their consequences for the planet. Scientists monitor ice loss, the behavior of marine life, and the impact of climate change on the region. The data collected in Antarctica contributes significantly to global climate models and helps predict the future of our planet.

The Protocol on Environmental Protection

The Madrid Protocol, which we mentioned in the previous segment, has played a central role in addressing contemporary environmental concerns. The protocol established the framework for environmental protection in Antarctica and has been followed by a series of annexes and agreements.

One of the most important annexes is the Protocol on Environmental Protection to the Antarctic Treaty, which entered into force in 1998. This protocol strengthens the commitment to preserving Antarctica's environment and designates the continent as a "natural reserve devoted to peace and science." It bans mining and sets strict rules for waste disposal, research activities, and the protection of ecosystems.

International Cooperation and Scientific Research

Antarctica remains a hub for international scientific cooperation. Research stations continue to be staffed by scientists from various countries, working together on a wide range of scientific disciplines. These collaborative efforts provide valuable insights into the planet's climate, biodiversity, and the impact of human activities.

Key research areas in Antarctica include the study of ice dynamics, climate change, oceanography, and the continent's unique ecosystems. Researchers work to unravel the mysteries of Antarctica's subglacial lakes, understand the behavior of the Southern Ocean, and monitor the health of penguin colonies and other wildlife.

The Ross Sea Region Marine Protected Area

One significant achievement in contemporary Antarctic history is the establishment of the Ross Sea Region Marine Protected Area (MPA). This MPA, which is one of the largest in the world, was created in 2016. It protects a vast area of the Southern Ocean and is designed to conserve the region's unique biodiversity and ecosystems. The MPA restricts commercial fishing and other potentially harmful activities.

The creation of the Ross Sea MPA is an example of international cooperation in preserving Antarctica's environment. It is a response to the increasing threat of overfishing and the need to safeguard the Southern Ocean's pristine waters.

Antarctica's Role in Global Climate Science

Antarctica continues to be a crucial region for climate science. The continent's ice sheets are key indicators of global climate change, and understanding their behavior is essential for predicting sea-level rise. In recent years, researchers have been able to use sophisticated techniques to measure ice mass changes with high precision.

The findings from Antarctica are a stark reminder of the consequences of human-induced climate change. The continent serves as a sentinel for the planet, emphasizing the urgency of addressing global warming and its effects.

Challenges and Pressing Issues

Antarctica faces numerous challenges in the 21st century. Chief among them is the increasing impact of climate change. The continent is warming at a rate much faster than the global average, resulting in the rapid retreat of glaciers, the loss of ice shelves, and a significant rise in sea levels. This warming has far-reaching consequences for the planet, as melting ice contributes to the potential for coastal flooding and significant disruptions to marine ecosystems.

Another pressing issue is the potential for increased human activity in Antarctica. While the Antarctic Treaty and its associated agreements have helped maintain the region's status as a place for peaceful scientific cooperation, there are concerns about potential resource exploitation and the need for sustainable management of the continent's unique ecosystems.

Antarctic Research Stations

Antarctica is home to numerous research stations operated by various nations. These stations serve as hubs for scientific exploration and are critical for understanding the region's climate, geology, and biodiversity. They are also the sites where researchers endure extreme conditions, working through the long Antarctic winters to collect valuable data.

Some of the most prominent research stations include the American McMurdo Station, the British Rothera Station, and the French-Italian Concordia Station. These stations are often characterized by their advanced scientific equipment, resilient structures designed to withstand harsh weather, and dedicated teams of scientists and support staff.

International Collaboration

One of the hallmarks of Antarctica's history is international collaboration. The Antarctic Treaty System, now including over 50 countries, sets the stage for peaceful cooperation and environmental protection in the region. The sharing of scientific data, logistics, and resources is fundamental to the success of research in Antarctica. The collaborative spirit that characterizes the continent serves as a model for international diplomacy and scientific discovery.

The Future of Antarctica

Looking ahead, the future of Antarctica is uncertain and holds both challenges and opportunities. The impact of climate change on the continent and its consequences for the rest of the world will continue to be a major focus of research. The role of Antarctica as an early warning system for global climate change emphasizes the urgency of addressing this critical issue.

The question of resource management is another concern. While the Antarctic Treaty prohibits mineral resource activities, there may be growing interest in the potential for sustainable fishing in the Southern Ocean. Balancing economic interests with environmental conservation will be a significant challenge for the region.

As technology advances, research in Antarctica will become increasingly sophisticated. The use of drones, remote sensing, and autonomous vehicles is revolutionizing our ability to study the continent. This technological progress will allow for more precise measurements and the exploration of previously inaccessible areas.

In conclusion, Antarctica's history is a testament to human exploration, scientific discovery, and international cooperation. This frozen continent, with its harsh conditions and stunning beauty, continues to be a focal point for understanding our planet and addressing some of the most pressing global challenges. As we move forward, it is essential to maintain the spirit of collaboration and environmental stewardship that has defined Antarctica's past and will shape its future.

Other Useful Information

Traveling to Antarctica is a unique and thrilling experience, offering the chance to explore this remote region's stunning landscapes and wildlife. Unlike traditional cruises, most Antarctic expeditions do not include onboard lodging for overnight stays. Instead, travelers are accommodated in specialized research stations, field camps, or comfortable expedition vessels.

Expedition Vessels

Expedition vessels are the primary mode of travel and accommodation for tourists visiting Antarctica. These ships are specially designed for polar exploration and offer a range of cabin categories, from cozy cabins to more spacious suites. Here's what you can expect from expedition vessel accommodations:

- **Cabin Types:** Cabins on expedition vessels come in various categories, often with different sizes and amenities. While standard cabins provide the essentials, higher-tier suites may offer more space, private balconies, and additional amenities.
- **Private Facilities:** All cabins typically have private en-suite bathrooms, ensuring your comfort and convenience during your journey.
- **Views:** Many cabins feature large windows or portholes, allowing you to enjoy the breathtaking Antarctic scenery from the comfort of your room.
- **Common Areas:** Expedition vessels also have common areas for socializing and relaxation, such as observation decks, lounges, and dining rooms.
- **Dining:** Meals are included in your expedition package and are served in a communal dining area. The culinary experience is designed to satisfy your appetite while accommodating dietary preferences.

- **Activities**: Expedition vessels offer a range of activities and lectures, enhancing your understanding of Antarctica's unique environment. You can also participate in shore landings and wildlife-watching excursions.

Research Stations and Field Camps

While expedition vessels are the primary means of accommodation for tourists, some expeditions offer the opportunity to visit research stations or field camps. These are more basic in terms of comfort but provide a unique experience:

- **Research Stations**: These are working scientific research facilities where you can interact with researchers and gain insight into their work. Accommodations are typically shared and may resemble dormitory-style lodging.

- **Field Camps:** Field camps are temporary accommodations set up for specific research projects. While staying at a field camp offers an authentic Antarctic experience, facilities are rudimentary, and travelers should be prepared for basic living conditions.

Booking and Preparation

When booking your Antarctic expedition, it's essential to consider the type of accommodation that best suits your preferences and budget. Expedition vessels offer the most comfortable and comprehensive experience, making them a popular choice for travelers. Research stations and field camps are typically reserved for those with a strong interest in scientific research or a desire for a more immersive experience.

Regardless of your choice, it's crucial to book your Antarctic expedition well in advance, as trips to this region have limited availability and can fill up quickly, especially during the peak travel season from November to March. Be prepared for the remote and challenging Antarctic environment by packing appropriate clothing and gear to ensure a safe and enjoyable experience.

In summary, accommodations in Antarctic port cities or towns differ significantly from traditional hotels and lodging options. Expedition vessels, research stations, and field camps offer unique and tailored experiences for travelers seeking to explore the pristine beauty of Antarctica while also contributing to scientific research and conservation efforts.

Customs Regulations on an Antarctica Cruise

When preparing for an Antarctica cruise, understanding customs regulations is crucial to ensure a seamless and hassle-free journey. While these regulations can vary based on your cruise itinerary and home country, here's a general overview to help you navigate customs procedures:

Documentation and Visas

Before embarking on your Antarctica cruise, it's essential to ensure you have the necessary travel documentation and visas:

- **Passport**: Make sure your passport is valid for at least six months beyond your intended return date. Check for any visa requirements for the countries you'll be transiting through or visiting on your way to Antarctica.

- **Visas:** Research the specific visa requirements for the countries included in your cruise itinerary. Many travelers to Antarctica enter through South American countries like Argentina or Chile, which may require tourist visas depending on your nationality. Ensure you have the correct visas well in advance of your journey.

Customs Declarations

As you travel to Antarctica, you'll likely have stopovers or embark from countries such as Argentina or Chile. It's crucial to understand the customs regulations for these transit countries:

- **Duty-Free Allowances:** Different countries have varying duty-free allowances for items like alcohol, tobacco, and personal belongings. Check with local customs authorities or your cruise line for specific limits. Be aware that exceeding these limits may require you to declare and potentially pay customs duties.

- **Valuables and Receipts**: To avoid complications during customs inspections, especially for high-value items such as expensive electronics, jewelry, or equipment, keep purchase receipts and documentation readily available. Some countries may require proof of ownership for certain items.

- **Currency:** While there are generally no restrictions on the amount of currency you can carry, certain countries may have rules about declaring larger sums of cash upon entry. Check the requirements for the specific countries you'll be visiting.

Antarctica is a pristine and delicate environment, and there are strict environmental regulations in place to protect its unique ecosystem:

- **Biosecurity Measures:** To prevent the introduction of non-native species, your clothing, equipment, and personal items may be subject to rigorous inspection and cleaning before disembarking in Antarctica. This is to minimize the risk of introducing any foreign organisms.

- **Waste Management:** Antarctica has strict waste disposal rules. Ensure you follow the guidelines provided by your cruise operator or research station to leave no trace and maintain the region's pristine condition.

Health Precautions

Before your Antarctica cruise, consider any health-related customs regulations:

- **Vaccinations**: Some countries or cruise operators may require specific vaccinations or medical clearances before allowing you to travel to Antarctica. Check the vaccination and health requirements for your specific itinerary.

Cruise-Specific Regulations

Each cruise operator may have its specific rules and regulations regarding customs and immigration procedures, as well as environmental protection guidelines. Be sure to familiarize yourself with these cruise-specific requirements.

In summary, preparing for customs regulations on an Antarctica cruise is essential to ensure a smooth and enjoyable journey. Research the requirements for your specific itinerary, carry the necessary documentation, and follow environmental and biosecurity guidelines to protect Antarctica's unique ecosystem.

Money Matters for Your Antarctica Cruise

When preparing for your Antarctica cruise, it's essential to consider the financial aspects of your journey. Antarctica is a unique destination with no native currency, so your financial planning will primarily revolve around your departure and return locations, which can vary widely depending on where you're traveling from.

Travel Funds and Payment Methods

Here are some key financial considerations for your Antarctica cruise:

- **Currency:** The currency you need will largely depend on the departure and return locations of your cruise. If you are departing from South American countries, such as Argentina or Chile, you might need Argentine Pesos (ARS) or Chilean Pesos (CLP) for expenses during your pre- or post-cruise stays. However, if you're departing from other locations, ensure you have the necessary currencies for those destinations.

- **ATMs and Credit Cards:** Access to cash through ATMs is essential. Ensure that your debit or credit cards work internationally and notify your bank of your travel plans to prevent any issues while abroad. Major credit cards like Visa, MasterCard, and American Express are widely accepted in many locations.

Travel Insurance

Travel insurance is vital for any international journey, but it's especially crucial when traveling to remote and challenging destinations like Antarctica. Make sure your travel insurance policy provides coverage for trip cancellations, delays, medical emergencies, and potential evacuation from Antarctica if needed. Check the policy's terms and conditions carefully to understand what is and isn't covered.

Environmental Regulations

While not directly related to currency, understanding and following environmental regulations is paramount when visiting Antarctica:

- **Biosecurity Measures:** Be prepared to adhere to strict biosecurity measures. This may include inspections and cleaning of your clothing, equipment, and personal items to prevent the introduction of non-native species into Antarctica's delicate ecosystem.

- **Waste Management:** Antarctica has stringent rules for waste disposal to preserve its pristine environment. Cruise operators and research stations will provide guidelines on responsible waste management during your visit.

In conclusion, thorough financial planning and compliance with environmental regulations are crucial for a successful and responsible Antarctica cruise. Regardless of your departure location, these considerations will help ensure a smooth and enjoyable expedition to this extraordinary part of the world.

Telephone and Communication in Antarctica

Staying connected during your Antarctica cruise is not just a matter of convenience but often a necessity. Antarctica's remote and challenging environment demands a specialized approach to communication. Here's a comprehensive guide:

- **Satellite Communication:** Antarctica's vastness and isolation mean that conventional cellular networks are virtually non-existent. Satellite communication is the backbone of connectivity in the region. Most expedition vessels in Antarctica are equipped with satellite communication systems. These systems provide internet access and the ability to make satellite phone calls. Keep in mind that satellite communication quality can vary based on your location within Antarctica. Expedition staff typically manage these systems, ensuring you can stay in touch with loved ones and access important information.

- **Emergency Communication:** Satellite phones play a crucial role in emergency situations. In the event of a medical emergency, equipment failure, or other urgent matters, a satellite phone is the fastest and most reliable way to communicate with rescue services or the cruise ship. Expedition staff, including medical professionals, carry satellite phones for this purpose.

- **Data Roaming:** Traditional data roaming services are not available in most parts of Antarctica due to the lack of cellular networks. Check with your mobile service provider to understand data roaming coverage in your departure and return locations. It's advisable to purchase an international data plan if offered by your provider.

- **Wi-Fi on Cruise Ships:** Many Antarctica cruise ships offer Wi-Fi services. However, the unique challenges of providing internet access in Antarctica, such as satellite-based connections and extreme weather conditions, can result in slow and expensive internet access. Bandwidth may be limited, and service interruptions can occur. It's best to manage your expectations regarding the quality and reliability of onboard Wi-Fi.

- **Local Antarctic Networks:** Some research stations and field camps in Antarctica have their own local networks, often used for scientific research, data transmission, and essential communications. However, these networks are typically isolated and not accessible to cruise passengers. Access to these networks is usually restricted to authorized personnel.

- **Time Zone:** Antarctica spans multiple time zones, with stations often adhering to the time zones of their home countries. The Antarctic Peninsula generally follows Chilean time (Chilean Standard Time, CLT, UTC-3). Your cruise operator will inform you of the timekeeping practices onboard the ship.

- **Environmental Considerations**: It's important to be aware that Antarctica is governed by strict environmental regulations to preserve its unique ecosystem. All communication infrastructure in the region is carefully managed to minimize its impact on the environment. This includes waste management practices for electronic equipment and restrictions on the use of radio frequencies that could interfere with wildlife or research.

In summary, staying connected in Antarctica is a unique challenge. Your options are primarily satellite-based, and internet access can be limited and costly. Be prepared for a different communication experience compared to more urban and connected destinations. Rely on the communication infrastructure provided by your cruise operator, and always respect the environmental regulations in place to protect this fragile ecosystem.

Visas and Residency for Travelers in Antarctica

Traveling to Antarctica is an adventure like no other, and understanding the visa and residency requirements for your expedition is crucial. While Antarctica is a unique destination with no permanent residents, it is governed by international treaties and agreements. Here's a comprehensive guide for travelers:

Visa Exemptions:

1. No Visa Requirement: Antarctica has no native population, and therefore, it does not have traditional visa requirements for tourists visiting the continent. Most travelers, including tourists and scientists, are not required to obtain a visa for their visit.

Travel Documentation:

2. Passport: While a visa is not required, a valid passport is necessary for travel to Antarctica. Ensure your passport is valid for at least six months beyond your intended departure date.

Permits for Entry:

3. Antarctic Treaty System: Entry to Antarctica is primarily managed through the Antarctic Treaty System, which regulates international relations in the region. Travelers typically need to secure permits through their tour operators or expedition leaders to visit specific sites on the continent. These permits are organized by your tour company and are essential for ensuring safe and sustainable travel.

Duration of Stay:

4. Temporary Visits: Tourist visits to Antarctica are temporary, often limited to the duration of your expedition or cruise. Visitors are not allowed to stay for an extended period or establish permanent residency.

Customs and Immigration:

5. Point of Entry: Travelers typically embark on an Antarctica expedition from one of the gateway cities, such as Ushuaia (Argentina) or Punta Arenas (Chile). Most expeditions include a pre-departure briefing and immigration checks in these cities. You'll need to comply with the customs and immigration requirements of the country you depart from.

Working in Antarctica:

6. Scientific Research: While tourists cannot work or establish permanent residency in Antarctica, researchers and scientists visiting the continent for research purposes must secure permits from their respective national authorities. These permits often involve compliance with environmental and safety regulations.

Environmental Regulations:

7. Environmental Protection: Antarctica is governed by strict environmental protection regulations. Travelers must adhere to these regulations to minimize their impact on the fragile ecosystem. This includes waste management practices, wildlife protection, and adherence to specific travel routes and visitor guidelines.

Understanding these regulations and requirements is essential for travelers to Antarctica. While it lacks traditional visa and residency procedures, responsible and sustainable tourism is vital for preserving this pristine environment. Always consult with your tour operator, expedition leaders, and relevant national authorities to ensure a smooth and legal travel experience.

Major Antarctica Cruise Ports

Antarctica, a continent of unparalleled beauty and pristine landscapes, welcomes travelers to its unique and remote ports of call. These ports are gateways to one of the most extraordinary and untouched regions on Earth, providing access to diverse wildlife, stunning ice formations, and scientific research stations. Here's a detailed overview of the major Antarctica cruise ports:

1. Ushuaia, Argentina:
- **Port Name**: Ushuaia Port at the southern tip of South America.
- **About:** Known as the "End of the World," Ushuaia is the world's southernmost city and the gateway to Antarctica.
- **Cruise Highlights**: Sail through the Beagle Channel, enjoy breathtaking views of the Andes, and visit the End of the World Museum.
- **Recommended Activities:** Explore Tierra del Fuego National Park, take a scenic train ride, and discover Ushuaia's vibrant dining scene.

2. Punta Arenas, Chile:
- **Port Name:** Punta Arenas' port is situated on the Strait of Magellan.
- **About:** Punta Arenas is a bustling city on the Patagonian plains, serving as a departure point for many Antarctica cruises.
- **Cruise Highlights**: Cross the legendary Strait of Magellan and sail through the beautiful fjords of southern Chile.
- **Recommended Activities:** Visit the historic Braun-Menéndez Palace, explore the Maggiorino Borgatello Museum, and embark on a tour to Torres del Paine National Park.

3. Stanley, Falkland Islands:
- **Port Name:** Stanley Port, the capital of the Falkland Islands.
- **About:** The Falklands are a British Overseas Territory in the South Atlantic, known for their stunning landscapes and rich wildlife.
- **Cruise Highlights:** Witness diverse bird species, including penguins, albatrosses, and cormorants.
- **Recommended Activities**: Explore Stanley's quaint streets, visit the Falkland Islands Museum, and enjoy wildlife-watching excursions to nearby islands.

4. South Georgia Island:
- **Port Name:** Grytviken, the administrative center of South Georgia.
- **About:** South Georgia is a remote and mountainous island in the southern Atlantic Ocean, famous for its wildlife.

- **Cruise Highlights:** Encounter vast colonies of king penguins, seals, and seabirds.
- **Recommended Activities:** Visit the whaling station museum, pay respects at Ernest Shackleton's grave, and hike to stunning viewpoints.

5. Paradise Bay, Antarctica:
- **Port Name:** Paradise Bay, a picturesque bay on the Antarctic Peninsula.
- **About:** Paradise Bay offers some of the most breathtaking scenery in Antarctica, with glaciers, icebergs, and pristine wilderness.
- **Cruise Highlights:** Witness magnificent ice formations, cruise alongside seals and whales, and explore research stations.
- **Recommended Activities:** Take a Zodiac cruise among icebergs, participate in kayaking adventures, and observe wildlife up close.

6. Port Lockroy, Antarctica:
- **Port Name:** Port Lockroy, a natural harbor on the Antarctic Peninsula.
- **About:** Port Lockroy is home to an active British research station and a museum.
- **Cruise Highlights:** Visit the famous Port Lockroy research station and its gift shop, and enjoy the scenic surroundings.
- **Recommended Activities:** Send postcards from the world's southernmost post office, learn about Antarctic research, and explore the stunning landscapes.

Each of these Antarctica cruise ports offers a unique opportunity to experience the natural wonders of the frozen continent, encounter its remarkable wildlife, and delve into its history of exploration and research. Your expedition to Antarctica will be a once-in-a-lifetime journey into a pristine and remote world.

Getting to Antarctica Cruise Ports

Reaching the remote and captivating cruise ports in Antarctica requires careful planning, considering the limited accessibility of this frozen wilderness. Here's a comprehensive guide on how to get to each of these extraordinary Antarctica cruise ports:

1. Ushuaia, Argentina:

- **By Air**: Your journey typically begins with a flight to Ushuaia's Malvinas Argentinas International Airport (USH), which serves as the primary gateway to Antarctica cruises.
- **By Land**: Ushuaia is located at the southern tip of South America, offering access by road if you're already in the region.

2. Punta Arenas, Chile:

- **By Air**: Flights to Presidente Carlos Ibáñez del Campo International Airport (PUQ) in Punta Arenas are common. From here, you'll continue your journey by sea to Antarctica.
- **By Land**: Punta Arenas is accessible by road, making it a starting point for overland expeditions.

3. Stanley, Falkland Islands:

- **By Air:** You'll likely fly to Mount Pleasant Airport (MPN) in the Falklands. Stanley, the capital, is just a short drive away.
- **By Sea:** Some expedition cruises to Antarctica include the Falklands as a stopover.

4. South Georgia Island:

- **By Sea:** South Georgia is primarily accessible by ship from other Antarctic locations, such as Ushuaia or Punta Arenas. It's a crucial stop on many Antarctica itineraries.

5. Paradise Bay, Antarctica:

- **By Sea:** You'll reach Paradise Bay by cruise ship. This remote destination is accessible only by water.

6. Port Lockroy, Antarctica:

- **By Sea:** Port Lockroy is part of many Antarctica cruise routes, and you'll arrive by ship. This remote post office and research station are accessible solely via the sea.

Your voyage to Antarctica is an unforgettable journey filled with stunning landscapes, abundant wildlife, and the thrill of exploration. Accessing these remote cruise ports involves careful coordination and the use of expedition vessels equipped for polar travel. Prepare to embark on the adventure of a lifetime as you explore the frozen frontier of Antarctica.

List of Major Cruise Lines

1. Quark Expeditions
  - Telephone: +1-802-490-1843
  - Website: [Quark Expeditions](https://www.quarkexpeditions.com/)

2. Hurtigruten
  - Telephone: +1-866-552-0371
  - Website: [Hurtigruten](https://www.hurtigruten.com/)

3. Lindblad Expeditions
  - Telephone: +1-800-397-3348
  - Website: [Lindblad Expeditions](https://www.expeditions.com/)

4. Abercrombie & Kent
  - Telephone: +1-630-954-2944
  - Website: [Abercrombie & Kent](https://www.abercrombiekent.com/)

5. Silversea Expeditions
  - Telephone: +1-888-978-4070
  - Website: [Silversea Expeditions](https://www.silversea.com/)

6. Oceanwide Expeditions
  - Telephone: +31-118-410 410
  - Website: [Oceanwide Expeditions](https://oceanwide-expeditions.com/)

7. Polar Latitudes
  - Telephone: +1-206-735-3328
  - Website: [Polar Latitudes](https://www.polarlatitudes.com/)

8. G Adventures
  - Telephone: +1-888-800-4100
  - Website: [G Adventures](https://www.gadventures.com/)

Please note that the availability of cruises may change, so it's a good idea to check their websites or contact them directly for the most up-to-date information, itineraries, and booking details.

Price Ranges of Antarctica Cruise Lines

1. Budget-Friendly Cruises:
  - **Price Range**: $5,000 to $7,000 per person for an 8 to 10-day cruise.
  - **Accommodation**: Inside or porthole cabins with basic amenities.
  - **Inclusions:** Most meals, guided shore excursions, and lectures by experts.
  - **Cruise Lines:** Oceanwide Expeditions, G Adventures, and Poseidon Expeditions.
  - **Details:** These budget-friendly cruises offer a more affordable way to explore Antarctica. While the cabins are comfortable, they are typically more modest. Meals are included, and you'll have the opportunity to participate in guided excursions to explore the pristine wilderness.

2. Mid-Range Cruises:
  - **Price Range:** $7,000 to $12,000 per person for an 8 to 12-day cruise.
  - **Accommodation:** Cabins with larger windows or private balconies, often with en-suite facilities.
  - **Inclusions:** All meals, guided excursions, educational programs, and some specialty activities.
  - **Cruise Lines:** Hurtigruten, Quark Expeditions, and Aurora Expeditions.
  - **Details:** Mid-range cruises strike a balance between cost and comfort. Cabins are more spacious and may offer additional amenities. These cruises often include educational programs, which add depth to the experience, and you can expect to enjoy a range of meals on board.

3. Luxury Cruises:
  - **Price Range:** $12,000 to $50,000+ per person for a 10 to 20-day cruise.
  - **Accommodation:** Suites with premium amenities, private balconies, and more space.
  - **Inclusions**: All-inclusive experiences with gourmet dining, top-shelf beverages, exclusive excursions, and luxury amenities.

- **Cruise Lines:** Silversea Expeditions, Seabourn, and Ponant.
- **Details:** Luxury Antarctica cruises offer unparalleled comfort and personal service. These all-inclusive cruises provide gourmet dining, premium beverages, and exclusive, immersive excursions, often with a team of expert naturalists.

Keep in mind that Antarctica cruise prices can vary due to factors such as the cruise's duration, the type of cabin, and the cruise line you choose. Always verify the most up-to-date pricing information directly with the cruise line, as costs may change over time. It's also essential to consider any additional costs, such as airfare to the embarkation point, travel insurance, and gear for the extreme Antarctic environment.

Additional Facts and Helpful Tips for Travelers

1. Weather and Climate:
- Antarctica is the coldest, driest, and windiest continent. Weather conditions can be highly unpredictable, with temperatures often dropping well below freezing.
- Summertime, from November to March, is the best time for cruises when temperatures are relatively milder (around 20°F to 40°F or -6°C to 4°C).
- Be prepared for rapid weather changes, and dress in layers to stay warm and dry.

2. Wildlife Encounters:
- Antarctica is a wildlife enthusiast's paradise. You can expect to see penguins, seals, whales, and numerous seabirds.
- Keep a respectful distance from wildlife to avoid disturbing their natural behavior.
- Photography enthusiasts should bring extra memory cards and battery backups since you'll likely take many pictures.

3. Packing Essentials:
- Pack warm, waterproof clothing, including insulated jackets, waterproof pants, and thermal layers.
- Don't forget high-quality waterproof boots for shore landings, as wet feet can lead to discomfort.

- Sunglasses, sunscreen, and lip balm with high SPF are essential to protect against the strong Antarctic sun.

4. Health Precautions:

- Get comprehensive travel insurance, including medical evacuation coverage, as medical facilities are limited in Antarctica.

- Consult with your doctor before the trip to ensure you're in good health, and bring any necessary medications.

- Seasickness can be a concern for some passengers. Consult with your healthcare provider regarding suitable remedies.

5. Adventure Activities:

- Some cruises offer adventurous activities such as kayaking, ice climbing, and camping. These activities often require advance booking and may have an additional cost.

- Check with your cruise operator for specific adventure options and availability.

6. Environmental Responsibility:

- Follow strict environmental guidelines while in Antarctica. Never disturb wildlife or leave any trace behind.

- Participate in conservation efforts, such as cleaning up litter found on shore.

- Do not remove rocks, plants, or any native Antarctic items as souvenirs.

7. Documentation and Permits:

- Ensure you have all the necessary travel documents, including your passport, visas, and cruise reservations.

- Antarctica cruises may require a permit, depending on your nationality. Check with your cruise operator for guidance on obtaining the required permits.

8. Photography Tips:

- Consider bringing a high-quality camera with a zoom lens to capture distant wildlife.

- Store your camera equipment in waterproof bags to protect against potential moisture exposure.

9. Astronomy Opportunities:

- Antarctica is one of the best places on Earth to view the night sky. Consider bringing binoculars or a telescope for stargazing.

10. Sea Sickness:
- The Drake Passage, a notoriously rough sea crossing, can lead to seasickness. Consult with your doctor about preventive measures or medications if you are prone to motion sickness.

11. Eco-Friendly Gear:
- Many cruise operators have eco-friendly gear available for guests, including reusable water bottles and insulated mugs. Consider bringing your own to reduce waste.

12. Local Culture:
- Although you'll primarily be focused on nature, it's interesting to note that Antarctica is governed by the Antarctic Treaty, a collaborative agreement for the peaceful use of the continent for scientific research.

13. Wi-Fi and Communication:
- Don't expect consistent Wi-Fi connectivity in Antarctica. Use this opportunity to disconnect from the digital world and immerse yourself in the breathtaking natural surroundings.

14. Safety Drills:
- Participate in safety drills and briefings conducted by the crew to ensure you are well-prepared for any unexpected situations.

15. Support for Research:
- Many Antarctica cruises support ongoing scientific research. Consider participating in research projects and contributing to our understanding of this unique environment.

These tips and facts should help you prepare for your Antarctica cruise, ensuring a safe, enjoyable, and responsible adventure in one of the world's most pristine and awe-inspiring destinations.

Printed in the USA
CPSIA information can be obtained
at www.ICGtesting.com
LVHW051956040124
767941LV00106B/5755